brood

Brood
© Kelly Granito / Cathexis Northwest Press

No part of this book may be reproduced without written permission
of the publisher or author, except in reviews and articles.

First Printing: 2025

ISBN: 978-1-952869-96-9

Cover by Jeff Guinn
Editing & Design by C. M. Tollefson
Cathexis Northwest Press
cathexisnorthwestpress.com

brood

poems by Kelly Granito

Cathexis Northwest Press

In *Brood*, Kelly Granito's virtuosic poems crack open the door of a family home into a mother's wry yet earnest heart as she navigates the all-too-often invisible odyssey of motherhood. When Granito's speaker takes on the persona of an editor requesting less Mary Oliver and more elegies for waves of rage you feel as you do the night feedings "we know we are in for unvarnished truth. With precise language and electrifying imagery, Granito's pieces tackle the nostalgic self-mythology of pre-parenthood years, the inescapable reminders of long-gone traumas and fears reignited by the desire to protect one's new "brood," and, ultimately, the difficulty in fusing past selves with a new one. At the same time, the toy trucks in Granito's verses take on the majesty of Neruda's tomatoes, a spouse's yard work ignites lust, and, weaving in and out of the entire collection, an acknowledgment of the transience of childhood provokes perpetual rumination *Brood* creates a fully authentic, human portrait through this mosaic of the psychic sensations in a mother's world. A stunning collection you simply cannot miss.

—Brigit Kelly Young is the author of several award-winning books for young adults. Her debut novel, *Worth a Thousand Words*, was a Junior Library Guild selection as well as a Best Book of 2019 from The Bank Street College of Education. Additionally, Ms. Young has published short fiction and poetry in journals like *The North American Review, 2 River View, Eclectica Magazine*, and *Burrow Press*, among others.

In *Brood*, Kelly Granito masterfully blends vivid nature imagery with complex reflections on motherhood. Hanging traps to kill visually stunning invasive beetles while quietly rooting for their larva to survive, she portrays herself as a morally ambiguous "executioner with paper lanterns," teaching her children about "the matter of dirty hands." She intertwines memories of wearing her mother's gold shoes on "Donna Summer nights" with the everyday act of gathering her children's scattered shoes while feeling lost at sea—ultimately surrendering to mornings where she must "look at the shoes and choose sharks." Yet, amid this tension, tiny moments of levity have the power to make "a photon / an inferno" that "calls us in like moths / again / and again."

—Denise Sedman is an award-winning poet and author of the poetry collection *The Past Isn't Done with Me Yet*. She has been published widely in literary journals and anthologies.

For Mom.

A poem is a gesture toward home.
— Jericho Brown

Table of Contents

Guidelines for mothers	1
Brood	2
Strawberries	3
Matrescence	4
Hydrangeas	5
Despite it all	6
Let Me Live Inside Your Love	7
Elegy for the bee that my children are covering with flowers	8
Japanese Beetles	9
No Mary	10
Morning Colors	11
An old classmate lives in Australia now	12
Hobby	13
Dinner performance	14
Oh, please	15
Rumble Strip	16
Pantoum for Totality	17
Wandering	18
Upon waking	19
Process	20
Good years	22

Guidelines for mothers

We ask that your poems
convey a coherent message
and achieve a high literary standard. Be a
thistle, sharp and flowery. Be a corpse
lily, entertaining and dark. Use sex
to break lines, or at least do something
to surprise us. Although we love
Mary Oliver, we don't want your best
Mary Oliver impressions. You're not all
soft animals: some of you are tilled earth
that long to be plowed
without being touched (sick as you are
of the communality of your breasts; the small
hands that grab them as if twisting corn
off a stalk; how when you lay on your back
awake they sink to your chest like sand
dollars and your husband never fails to find one
in his sleep like it's you he dreams of
scooping into a bucket at low tide).
We need more from you
about regret—more elegies for waves
of rage you feel as you do the night
feedings. There's no need to announce
your heart—just show us
the only small and soiled thing left
to wash, fold, and toss in a pile. If you do nothing
else, please tackle hard hitting themes
in your submission.

Brood

It's the Armageddon
of sound...Triassic fireworks
spew from the ground, buzz like cables
ripped from a pole in a thunderstorm.

The brood before last I was seventeen: all spit
and no fire. I longed to be ripped
from my skin like a creature escaping
its molted bones; prayed

for my shame to become a spring
jacket one might simply unzip and remove.
And the brood before that, I was fresh
from the womb. If they were out there

butchering maples, I didn't notice.
But in these years of homebound
mothering; the constant spinning
in place like a recluse

spider—oh, I pine for those lost shells
that cling to the porch steps...little ghosts
scattered in the yard. I long to happen
upon one, crouch down and trace

with the tip of my finger the sudden split
where the being erupted—a nymph
no longer—hellbent on sapling slaughter
(really, they don't mean to plunder

the branches, they just need a place
to abandon their eggs...just for a moment,
not noticing the leaves have turned
to brown fluttering flags of defeat).

Either way they leave us screaming
as we cover our ears, eyes to the sky
desperate, now, to sneak cicadas
into every poem.

Strawberries

Something died that summer
the strawberries didn't come in,
save a few unripe white droplets
under wet leaves. In the garden
the cucumbers spread like sickness
among toddlers before being swallowed
by mildew, and the weeds went wild
between the deck's wooden slats,
sun-warped with underuse.

From somewhere down there
the smell came quickly—hot,
sickly—pulled at our stomachs
like ropes towing wagons of grief.
We held our breath and tossed water
balloons at the kids all dripping
with laughter, oblivious
to whatever had gone bad,
as something tore away from us like squirrels
startled from the garden bed…tangled, still,
in leftover vines.

Matrescence

Some mornings
I toss like a skiff in a cyclone
of bedding until five thirty,
then appear in the hallway
as if emerging from a three hour
matinee: thrown by the light
and wondering what year it is.

I discover a chore—
shoes on the bottom step; pour
their playground contents
down the kitchen sink
and for a moment I am stolen
by the rosy dawn spreading
like a bruise above the neighbor's roof.

I think of Robert Redford
in the film about the mariner
lost at sea with a failed motor, sharks circling
as he bobs in silence for an hour
and forty minutes. Gone in it,
I turn on the disposal. Chomp,
sputter, silence.

So much for movies
where the woman sails a smooth
matrescence: these poems,
once charted in sky,
now whiz around my chest like pebbles
congesting a faithful engine.

Some mornings I look at the shoes and choose
sharks.

Hydrangeas

This woman is a doctor
who hotfoots stroke victims
through the thrashing wings
of an emergency room at midnight,
then bikes home to plate her children's
Belgian waffles with whipped cream. I pour cereal
and write poems, duty-bound
only to the slickness of milk
and words…and still I run
myself into the ground most days.

How do I tell her
I spend midnights attending the call
of field crickets; saving no lives
but my own? Then again,
we are none of us faithful
to any one nature
of healing—
perhaps she too notices the pale blue blossoming
of a hematoma and thinks: *hydrangeas.*
Perhaps poetry makes the bedside
rounds in the end.

Despite it all

Conspicuous as a black bear
behind a birch tree,

the longing I still have for you
roves loudly through

the universe
of photos I took while you slept in:

>[spider
>wrapping our stove light in silk]
>
>[wishbone
>drying on our windowsill]
>
>[steam
>collecting on the pane]
>
>[heart
>traced into the steam]
>
>[double-yoked egg
>hard-boiled and sliced in half]
>
>[list
>on our fridge: plums, honey]

the one I posted:

>[lingering moon]
>
>*Still your satellite.*

Let Me Live Inside Your Love

of trucks, where your fire engine saves me
a seat among the Hot Wheels,
who hitch a ride on its ladder and zoom
home to their bin across your bedroom
floor. Where your boom lift cranks
its sturdy arm to reach my electric heap
of a heart and tenderly straightens
my jumbled wires.
                      Let me retreat
to last year, when you held your friend's face and fell
to the ground laughing as his skid steer jammed
your dump truck full of dead leaves
and broken sticks. Please,

                let me fall asleep
inside your colossal love of trucks,
where you sing to them, now, beneath
the bedside light—but it's me
who listens. Let me borrow your eyes
to see the garbage truck like you do; rejoice
from the window as it crushes junk in the violet
light of morning; clap as it lumbers through its own fumes
and flips our waste into its belly like a happy bear
gobbling fish. I don't know how it lives so well
on our souring refuse, but I know your sweet ovation
must surely fuel its daily pledge to clear the curb
of yesterday's mess.

Elegy for the bee that my children are covering with flowers

While the drones were busy
thrusting their genes

to the queen like hymns
to a god,

did this worker kneel
quiet as afternoon

prayer and prep her cell
for its next dweller?

In my six years playing host
to little night visitors

from down the hall, I too know sleep
comes only with the gold smoke

of dawn across my face.
Poor thing

probably allowed herself at last
to close her eyes

and drift toward that colony
of small hands

coming now to forge her
mausoleum

of petals, then eased
into her plummet

to our deck, pleased
to have saved the swarm

the trouble of her body.

Japanese Beetles

Well shit. They're back at it
in the torch lilies: two stacked emeralds
under copper wings, iridescent
as bubbles; with peacock plume
antennas and those telltale ivory
tufts that speckle their bellies
like soft ellipses…

                   my heart broke
in June, not yet knowing their name
but knowing elaborate and dazzling
creatures are never native to this
zone's earth-toned lack
of imagination, and my gardener
husband says I must kill them all.

Torch lilies, too.

I accept the science of this; educate
our children in the matters of this
and make sure they bear witness.
And as with most of my generation's clamoring
for gold stars, I am exhausted
by the performance of this.

                  I reach deep
into what's left of my garden this late
in summer, root around for a place to hang
traps—an executioner
with paper lanterns—but really I root
for their larva to beat me
to the punch; to overwinter in our shared
world's fertile crust, sequestered
in the sanctuary of my small rebellion
so come April I may instruct
my own children in the matter
of dirty hands.

No Mary

Truth is, I don't care for gardening. I'm no Mary
quite contrary with her sea oddities
arranged in dirt. I just like watching you
do it—run the wheelbarrow here and there, run your hands
over jasmine, kneel to earth to deadhead
roses. Come summertime,
come autumn leaves, come winter's biting
moon

spring comes
as easily as I fall back in love with you
and the passing rains that coax us
into bloom.

Morning Colors

Open the news   scroll   scroll   scroll   it's all a waking
nightmare of course, and like all of us I'm afraid
I'm hooked...then I notice the flag ceremony
unfolding on the snow-
cloaked black
top

where I just deposited my eldest—a child in braids
makes clouds with her breath; her bare hands
yank the halyard and send
skyward shocks
of glory
red

that breach white like first light breaks a night
blizzard, then flutter dumbly under stars
on an acquiescent pole—
an obstinate cardinal;
a winter
stick.

How easily we teach them to fold grief
into ever-smaller triangles
to shove in a drawer
when gone
the sun;
bend

to that which keeps us
on a rope, so
long as the
friction

warms our
hands.

An old classmate lives in Australia now

and I don't know how much longer
I can endure her dispatches
from the sunny side: her children safe
in wide-brimmed hats, their constant summer
trips down red roads hugged by gum
trees

while in this timeline
I've collected myself like a porch plant
brought in from the cold; rolled
my towels into pastel snakes
to place beneath the windows
as my own kids lose rights
like teeth and watch
Bluey.

*In these times I can't think
of a better place to live*, she writes
beneath a photo of a beach. Briefly,
I consider slamming into her
DMs; demanding she answer
to her audacity, which is another way of saying
the audacity of the country she fled.

Instead, I double-tap with the mild irritation
you might reserve for a lover
who sleeps in as you fold laundry
at the foot of the bed, listening for wisps
of unexpected wisdom in their dream-mutterings.

Hobby

My therapist said hobbies help
ease the transition, so my hands
work these strings like a six-month old
getting the hang of a spoon. Nothing

has eased: I'm sick, always—
throat an exhaust pipe, heart
a mouse trap, nipples cashed
by our third earsplitting baby.

I grip the neck and pick to the warble
of fledglings in their nest in the eaves;
convince myself in my fevered sleep
deprivation they are crying for me.

Later I do dishes, throw out the leftovers
and wipe the year from my brain
as these chords fill my head like cotton
in a medicine jar, muffling

the rattling capsules
while the finches whistle
in their shit outside.

Dinner performance

for our young
audience: jokes
skipped across our table

like sandstones—*please pass
the spider feet. Who
just farted?* Giggles

from our middle
child, who ripples
tepid hearts. Now,

sparks
call us in
like moths

who believe
a photon
an inferno;

who trust
powder wings
to carry them

again
and again.

Oh, please

They tell us the years are short
                but the years in this house
        feel as short as the days
                feel like dogs: a good boy
no longer keeps watch at the window
                or begs me for bones.
I'm free to bat at the weeks like ribbons
                of light sweeping the floor,
    knock months off our dresser
                as seasons march like ants
    towards infinity. Without hands
                offering treats, I return to the woods
a hunter. Still, if you wait at the edge
                of night I'm likely to appear
      on our porch steps hungry
                and quiet as the moon; push
      my head against your palm
               and do the work myself,
    grateful. To forfeit eight lives
                to share this one with you
    and then slink soundlessly
                into the wet grass of daybreak—
these poems limp and gasping
                tokens of worship left at your feet.

Rumble Strip

I nearly killed us all last night while driving home.
Aloof as it remains at bedtime, sleep rolls right up
like a semi-truck when my kids are dead
to the world in their car seats,
hands at rest on whatever soiled animal carried them

to their dreams. I blamed the thrum
of vehicles, white noise of my childhood
cradled by interstate…but really I was trailing
those dotted white lines of memory:
my children

on one side, road trips of my youth
on the other—Dad with his hands
at 10 and 2, mostly lost
in the radio. Mom facing the onslaught
of guilt with her eyes closed.

Everything that matters is here
in the dark, guard railed by the bumps that keep us
among the conscious

while the rest passes quiet
as clouds on the shoulder

toward exits unknown.

Pantoum for Totality

Standing the driveway with my daughter, eclipse glasses
affixed to the sky, we track the moon.
A hundred kids your age were killed by a missile today,
I think. *We've gotten nowhere.*

Affixed to the sky, we track the moon.
She encircles the sun with her cheerio.
I think: we've gotten nowhere.
The moon shifts into position above us.

My child eclipsing sunlight with cereal
will never toil in hunger's curved shadow.
The moon shifts into position above us.
We clear our schedules

to race to the path of its curved shadow
for a moment more fleeting than each of our lives;
we clear our schedules
for stardust

while in a moment as fleeting as each of our lives
A hundred children were killed
over stardust,
as we stand in the driveway and wait.

Wandering

We reach for each other
with the obliquity of two sugar pines

that reach for sky: stalwarts of old
growth, secretly slanting

into whatever path offers each
the clearest view of the sun.

We forget our braided
roots will keep us

forever in cahoots,
while in the wind we wave

a wordless, years-long
goodbye.

Upon waking

As usual, a rat
scuttled into our garage
as if skating a frozen pond
on crooked feet: lunged from plywood
shelves; struck the van's
dented hood and hung
from that bulb that punches
a single treasured hole
of light in our homestead's
boxed heart.

We should kill it,
I whispered. *Catch and release,*
you countered—but then,
guts. In my hands, your heavy red-
handled shovel, slick
with blood and entrails
cast to the wall like snow
to the curb on nightlike
winter mornings.

The rest is gone
except for your shovel, your tender
scraping of pavement.
How you carried it
to the driveway while I sulked
in the idling van. How I watched
in the rearview mirror
as you carved a gentle clearing
to daybreak.

Process

Near the robin's egg
house where I grew up neighbored
by highway in every direction,

seven pines in a line
still shoulder a truce
between 23-South and two swing sets.

It's mid-July. I'm here
with my son—all umber
eyes and halfway sprouted

permanent teeth—he knows
more of this world, somehow,
than he's seen. Still,

against the sky he spots the flame-stained
wings of a monarch. *Homebound
from Mexico to breed*, I say.

> *That's like what you did, mom, that spring
> when I was in your belly: left New York
> and came back here to have me where your parents had you.*

Then it pounces: my backbiting
impulse to reveal things
I think he hasn't noticed—dead butterflies

and trash in the grass; gold flashes
that masquerade as lightning
bugs bewitched by twilight beyond

the pines: just timber trucks ripping by
at 80 mph. I remember I don't want him
coming here alone.

> *You forgot the most amazing thing about Northern Michigan*
> *monarchs is when they fly south over Lake Superior*
> *they swing a sudden left and fly east*
>
> *for a while, then south again*
> *and scientists think they must sense something*
> *that once blocked the path of their ancestors.*

I bring the soft thunder
of the highway like a shell
to my ear and listen

for a gone mountain.
And he swings—lifts his feet
and gifts his weight to the foxtrot

of momentum and gravity,
coasts on this energy
of motion like monarchs

over lakeshore,
too high to be seen
from the ground as the sun

shatters itself on waves beneath them.

And this—

this is the way these poems
unfurl from silk swaddles
of hope that hang along the underside

of sorrow, then lift to the page, carried
on winds of sudden gratitude.

That is amazing, I say before thanking
the pines for growing right
where they were planted by some idiot in the sixties;

for doing what they could to keep me alive.

Good years

You said
they are like trees
along the highway, blurred
by our haste. Perhaps they were
the years you fell in love with yourself; those
blue eye-shadow years—years of shimmering rose
gold wedges making love to your ankles. You traipsed
down Broadway twenty blocks in those Donna Summer
weekends with Fawn on the east-side years; those bad-
girl in the tight cobalt dress years. I think of you now, in
my rushing through another drop-off years, my years
of setting up calls. I'm settling into my Trazadone-
at-bedtime years while on my lap my own sweet
child smiles up from her amnesia
years—she won't remember
this.
I'm in my jeans
strangling my gut years: half of me
erupting over a ruthless button, the other half
dismissed into softness beneath. My hourglass
years; sand in a pile. Didn't I find those gold heels
buried in the dress-up box? I strapped them on and
shuffled around the unfished basement, pretending
to be you. The years now seem to loop over each
other like laces tied by a child who pulls together
bunny ears. From my window this town echoes
lights on the river; skyline thins to billboards
and trees as I rush home to embed myself
in her memories. I know I will not return
from the loss of these years,
and knowing is what
makes them
good.

Some of these poems, and earlier versions of them, were first published in the following journals and anthologies: The Emerson Review, the Louisville Review, Iron Horse Review, Gramercy Review, Burrow Press, Santa Clara Review, Ibis Head Review, and Noctua Review.

First and foremost, thank you to my beautiful brood, Otis, Melody, and Desmond: without you these poems, and this life for which I am so grateful, would not exist. I love each of you endlessly.

Alex, thank you—for our brood, but also for your steadiness, your tenderness, your quick wit, your insanely green thumbs, and your unrelenting generosity, all of which show up between the lines in these poems. I love you immeasurably and am forever grateful for it all. Bread and roses.

I owe an extreme debt of gratitude to the highly skilled childcare providers and teachers who make it possible for me to work and write. This book would not exist without them.

Thank you, C.M. and Cathexis Northwest, for making this process exciting and easy.

Jeff, thank you for the beautiful cover. You nailed it.

Chad and Brigit, thank you for letting me fire off first drafts of these poems in the middle of your respective work days, allowing my words to settle and gestate in kind, supportive hearts.

Megan and Evan, thank you for so many years of laughter and camaraderie. Our bond is the reason mine is a brood of three.

Thank you, Dad, for the pet lizards, turtles, and hermit crabs, the pond and fishing expeditions, and the gardens of my childhood. You nurtured my forever-love of nature.

Mom: you always said I'd understand when I had my own kids. You were right—about that, and about all things in life that really matter. Thank you.

Kelly Granito is a poet, educator, and naturalist from Ann Arbor, Michigan, where she lives with her husband, kids, cat, and too many plants. Her poetry has been featured in the Emerson Review, Iron Horse Review, the Louisville Review, Burrow Press, Midwestern Gothic, and many other journals.

Also Available from Cathexis Northwest Press:

Something To Cry About
by Robert Krantz

Suburban Hermeneutics
by Ian Cappelli

God's Love Is Very Busy
by David Seung

that one time we were almost people
by Christian Czaniecki

Fever Dream/Take Heart
by Valyntina Grenier

The Book of Night & Waking
by Clif Mason

Dead Birds of New Zealand
by Christian Czaniecki

The Weathering of Igneous Rockforms in High-Altitude Riparian Environments
by John Belk

If A Fish
by George Burns

How to Draw a Blank
by Collin Van Son

En Route
by Jesse Wolfe

sky bright psalms
by Temple Cone

Moonbird
by Henry G. Stanton

southern athiest. oh, honey
by d. e. fulford

Bruises, Birthmarks & Other Calamities
by Nadine Klassen

Wanted: Comedy, Addicts
by AR Dugan

They Curve Like Snakes
by David Alexander McFarland

the catalog of daily fears
by Beth Dufford

Shops Close Too Early
by Josh Feit

Vanity Unfair and Other Poems
by Robert Eugene Rubino

Destructive Heresies
by Milo E. Gorgevska

Bodies of Separation
by Chim Sher Ting

The Night with James Dean and Other Prose Poems
by Allison A. deFreese

About Time
by Julie Benesh

Suspended
by Ellen White Rook

The Unempty Spaces Between
by Louis Efron

Quomodo probatur in conflatorio
by Nick Roberts

Suspended
by Ellen White Rook

Call Me Not Ishmael but the Sea
by J. Martin Daughtry

Wild Evolution
by Naomi Leimsider

Coming To Terms
by Peter Sagnella

Acta
by Patrick Wilcox

Honeymoon Shoes
by Valyntina Grenier

Practising Ascending
by Nadine Hitchiner

Home Visit
by Michal Rubin

LA CIUDAD EN TI: THE CITY WITHIN YOU
by Karla Marrufo
Translated from the Spanish by Allison A. deFreese

Resin in the Milky Way
by Amanda Rabaduex

Bone Hunting
by Trinity Catlin

Muskets for the Bear Problem
by Andrew Whitmer

Self-Portraits as a Reddening Sky
by Samuel Gilpin

Desert
by Eric Larsh

Leaving the Religion of Self-Harm
by Bailey Blumenstock

Fractured Symphony
by Andi Myles

La dulzura de los naufragios: The Sweetness of Shipwrecks
by Karla Marrufo
Translated from the Spanish by Allison A. deFreese

Love & Fear
by Henry G. Stanton

Sunlight Later
by Jo Matthews

The Longed For Longer For
by Sibani Sen

Bleeding Ghosts
by Lara Chamoun

As Jaguars Dreamed On The Earth's Dark Face
by Clif Mason

Cathexis Northwest Press

www.ingramcontent.com/pod-product-compliance
Lightning Source LLC
Chambersburg PA
CBHW060543080526
44586CB00012B/840